Brazil

by Shirley W. Gray

Content Adviser: Professor Sherry L. Field,
Department of Social Science Education, College of Education,
The University of Georgia

Reading Adviser: Dr. Linda D. Labbo,
Department of Reading Education, College of Education,
The University of Georgia

COMPASS POINT BOOKS

Minneapolis, Minnesota

Compass Point Books
3722 West 50th Street, #115
Minneapolis, MN 55410

Visit Compass Point Books on the Internet at *www.compasspointbooks.com* or e-mail your request
to *custserv@compasspointbooks.com*

Photographs ©: Visuals Unlimited/Jeff Greenberg, cover; International Stock/Paolo Fridman, 4; Visuals Unlimited/Gilbert L. Twiest, 6; Manfred Gottschalk/Tom Stack and Associates, 7; Haroldo De Faria Castro/FPG International, 8; Spencer Grant/FPG International, 9; Eduardo Garcia/FPG International, 10; Photri-Microstock, 11; Visuals Unlimited/Kiell B. Sandved, 12; David Liebman, 13; Tom and Therisa Stack/Tom Stack and Associates, 14; International Stock/Paolo Fridman, 15; Visuals Unlimited/M. and D. Long, 16; Visuals Unlimited/George Loun, 17; Inga Spence/Tom Stack and Associates, 18 top; Joe McDonald/Tom Stack and Associates, 18 bottom; Photophile/Gary Gaugler, 19; Lee Foster/FPG International, 20; Haroldo De Faria Castro/FPG International, 21; North Wind Picture Archives, 23; Photophile/Gary Gaugler, 24; International Stock/Donna Carroll, 25; North Wind Picture Archives, 26, 27, 28; Unicorn Stock Photos/Jeff Greenberg, 29; Reuters/Ruy Baron/Archive Photos, 30; Unicorn Stock Photos/Jeff Greenberg, 31; Photophile/Jeff Greenberg, 32; Visuals Unlimited/P. Perron, 33; International Stock/Paolo Fridman, 34; Index Stock Imagery, 35; Tony Generico/FPG International, 36; Trip/F. Nichols, 37; Haroldo Castro/FPG International, 38; International Stock/Paolo Fridman, 39; Photri-Microstock, 40; Lloyd Harvey/FPG International, 41; Luis Rosendo/FPG International, 42; Spencer Grant/FPG International, 43; Norman Owen Tomalin/Bruce Coleman, Inc., 45.

Editors: E. Russell Primm and Emily J. Dolbear
Photo Researcher: Svetlana Zhurkina
Photo Selector: Dawn Friedman
Design: Bradfordesign, Inc.
Cartography: XNR Productions, Inc.

Library of Congress Cataloging-in-Publication Data
Gray, Shirley W.
    Brazil / by Shirley W. Gray.
      p. cm. — (First reports)
    Includes bibliographical references and index.
    Summary: An introduction to the geography, history, culture, and people of the largest country
in South America.
    ISBN 0-7565-0027-3
      1. Brazil—Juvenile literature. [1. Brazil.] I. Title. II. Series.
    F2508.5 .G72 2000
    981—dc21

                                       00-008524

Table of Contents

"Bom Dia!"

"*Bom dia!* Good day! Welcome to Brazil."

You might hear this greeting if you visit Brazil. It is the largest country on the **continent** of South America. Brazil covers almost half of South America.

▲ *Brazilian children*

▲ Map of Brazil

Most of Brazil lies south of the **equator**. The equator is an imaginary line around the middle of the Earth. The equator crosses the northern part of Brazil.

The borders of Brazil touch ten other countries
in South America. The entire eastern side of Brazil
lies along the Atlantic Ocean. Most people in Brazil
live within 200 miles (322 kilometers) of the Atlantic

▲ *São Paulo*

▲ *Rio de Janeiro*

Ocean. São Paulo is the largest city in Brazil. It is on the southeastern coast. Rio de Janeiro is another large city on the coast.

The Land of Brazil

▲ *The Atlantic Forest near Rio de Janeiro*

Brazil has many different kinds of land. It has rain forests and jungles. It has wooded **lowlands** and rich farmland called **highlands**. Brazil also has flat land called **plains**.

The Central Highlands is a large **plateau** in south-eastern Brazil. A plateau is a high area of flatland with steep sides. Coffee, an important crop, grows here. Coffee plants thrive in the plateau's rich soil, warm temperature, and regular rainfall.

▲ *Coffee seedlings are grown in these open-air buildings.*

In the south, the Central Highlands give way to a wide plain called the **pampa**. The land here is perfect for raising crops and animals. This area is also home

▲ Wheat fields

▲ *Gauchos herding cattle*

to the **gaucho**, the South American cowboy. Gauchos ride around on horseback. A gaucho wears a silver belt, baggy pants, and a cape called a poncho.

The lowlands are in the north and west, around the Amazon River. This area has the largest rain forest in the world.

The Amazon River

▲ *The Amazon River*

The Amazon River is the second-longest river on the Earth, after the Nile River in Africa. The Amazon is a powerful river with hundreds of branches. It flows from the Andes Mountains in Peru across Brazil to the Atlantic Ocean.

The Amazon River is the largest in the world in terms of how much

▲ *A pirarucu*

water it holds. One fifth of all the freshwater flowing into oceans comes from the Amazon.

Scientists think that as many as 3,000 kinds of fish live in the freshwater of the Amazon River. For example, the pirarucu may be the world's largest freshwater fish. It weighs up to 275 pounds (125 kilograms)! The piranha also lives in the Amazon River. It is a meat-eating fish that usually eats other fish. Sometimes, when they are in a feeding frenzy, piranhas attack humans or other large animals.

▲ A red piranha

A World inside the Rain Forest

During the year, heavy rains soak the lowland forests near the Amazon River. These rains make trees grow. One of these trees—brazilwood—helped give Brazil its name.

Millions of kinds of plants and animals live in the Amazon rain forest. Scientists have

▲ *The Amazon River flowing through forests*

▲ *Brazil nuts*

not even discovered all these living things yet. The
top branches of the tallest trees form a leafy ceiling
called a canopy. Many animals live here too.

The most common creatures in the forest are spiders and insects. In the rain forest, tiny leafcutter ants climb trees that are 100 feet (31 meters) tall. The ants cut the leaves into small pieces and carry them back down to their homes. Sometimes the forest floor is alive with the moving leaves.

▲ *Leaf-cutter ants*

Other animals in the forest are sloths, jaguars, and capybaras. The sloth spends most of its life in the trees. Here it blends with the leaves and branches and hides from its enemy—the jaguar. Large rodents called capybaras live near the rivers and streams. They weigh

▲ A three-toed sloth

A capybara ▶

up to 145 pounds (66 kilograms)—about as much as a grown person!

Because of the constant rain and warm temperatures, many trees in the rain forest are evergreens. Hundreds of kinds of birds, including parrots and toucans, live in these trees. Other types of animals, such as monkeys, depend on the trees for shelter and food.

▲ *A toucan*

Protecting the Rain Forest

▲ *Bare hills show the destruction of the rain forest.*

In recent years, the trees in the rain forest have become a way for people to make money. During the 1970s, many people moved to the Amazon lowlands to cut down trees. Some people wanted to sell the wood. Others wanted to grow crops on the land.

Thousands of acres of trees in the rain forest have been destroyed. Many animals lost their homes.

The rain forests are important to the whole world. Some of the plants found there are used in medicine to fight diseases. Maybe someday a plant found in the rain forest will help cure cancer. The rain forest also provides food such as bananas, Brazil nuts, and cocoa for chocolate.

▲ *Cutting down trees in the rain forest*

The Brazilian government passed laws to protect the rain forest. One important law prevents anyone from selling wood from the rain forest to other countries. Today, the government uses satellites to watch the rain forest. The United States and other countries help the Brazilians protect the rain forests.

Native Americans

The first people in Brazil were Native Americans. They were hunters and farmers. In the 1400s, Europeans explored and settled in Brazil. Some Native Americans lived near the coast where the Europeans settled. Many died because of diseases brought by Europeans. Others died of overwork. Some learned European ways to farm and live.

The Native Americans who lived in the rain forests had little contact

▲ *A Brazilian native with a zarabatana, or shooting tube*

▲ *A traditional leader in the Yaguan tribe*

with the early Europeans. They lived as they always had.

Today, more than 200 groups of Native Americans still live in Brazil. Most of them live in central or northern Brazil.

The Native Americans in the rain forests have trouble earning a living today. Although the rain forest has lush

▲ *A village along the Amazon River*

trees, fruits, and flowers, it does not have good soil for farming. Many people still live as their grandparents did. They hunt, fish, and gather food in the forests.

A Mixture of People

In 1500, explorer Pedro Álvares Cabral claimed Brazil for Portugal. Then he sent a ship filled with brazil-wood to Europe. From then on, the land that produced this valuable wood was called Brazil. The Portuguese began to build colonies there.

▲ A Brazilian port in the 1700s

▲ *A coffee plantation in southern Brazil*

The Portuguese built large farms in Brazil. They grew sugarcane and coffee. They brought slaves from Africa to work on the farms. In 1822, Brazil won its independence from Portugal. The people formed their own government. In 1888, the slaves were freed. They remained in Brazil.

▲ *African slaves were brought to Brazil to pick coffee.*

Today, Brazilians are a rich mixture of Native Americans, Europeans, Africans, and Asians. Most of the Europeans who settled other countries in South

▲ Members of a local soccer team on the beach in Rio de Janeiro

America spoke Spanish. However, the official language of Brazil is Portuguese. French and English are the main second languages for educated Brazilians. There are more than 100 other Native American languages spoken in Brazil.

▲ Brazil's president, Fernando Henrique Cardoso, with soccer star Pelé in 1999

Almost 170 million people live in Brazil. It is the fifth-largest country in the world. The country is made up of twenty-six states and a federal district. Brasília is the capital of Brazil. The head of Brazil's government is the president. He or she is elected by the people.

Because Brazil lies south of the equator, its seasons are the opposite of countries that lie north of the equator. For example, June and July are winter months. But most of Brazil is tropical, which means it

▲ Famous Ipanema Beach in Rio de Janeiro is warm in winter and summer.

is warm year-round. In June, the temperatures are around 75° Fahrenheit (24° Celsius). During the summer months of January and February, the temperatures are around 84° Fahrenheit (29° Celsius). Brazilians can wear short-sleeved shirts all year!

Brazilians also enjoy outdoor sports throughout the year. Soccer is the most popular sport. Most

▲ *Maracana Stadium in Rio de Janeiro holds 20,000 soccer fans.*

▲ *Young soccer players in a small village*

children learn to play soccer when they are young.
Fans around the world know Pelé, Brazil's great soccer
player. Brazilian children also like basketball, volley-
ball, mountain biking, and swimming.

Food

▲ *Brazilian meals are varied and colorful.*

A meal in Brazil usually includes black beans, rice, beef, vegetables, and fruit. Brazilians also eat a root called manioc. A favorite dish is *feijoada*, a stew made of beans, meat, and chili peppers, served over rice.

▲ *Grilled meat is a favorite dish in Brazil.*

To make *churrasco*, chunks of beef are roasted outdoors over a fire. It is a popular dish in south Brazil. The gauchos cook all their meat this way. A popular dessert served in Brazil is *cocada branca*. It is made from coconut, milk, and sugar and served with fresh fruit.

Religion

The Portuguese settlers brought Christianity to Brazil. Most of them were Roman Catholics. Today, most Brazilians are Catholic.

▲ *An Easter Sunday procession outside a church in Ouropreto*

The African slaves who were brought to Brazil had a religion called *candomblé*. But the Europeans did not allow the Africans to practice their own religion. They forced the slaves to go to Catholic Church. The slaves pretended to pray like the Christians but they prayed to their own gods. For example, they prayed to Oxala —their god of the harvest.

▲ *A candomblé priestess*

▲ These women attend a Japanese Buddhist temple in São Paulo.

After slavery ended in 1888, the Africans were free to pray as they wished. Today, many Brazilians take part in candomblé ceremonies.

Celebrations and Music

In the summer, people in Brazil dance to music during a celebration called Carnaval. Carnaval is Brazil's biggest festival. People enjoy music, parades, and dancing in the streets. Carnaval begins three days before the Christian season of Lent. In Rio de Janeiro on New Year's Eve, the people go to the beach

▲ People crowd the streets during Carnaval.

▲ Elaborate floats are part of a Carnaval parade.

for a midnight party with candles.

Music and dance are always part of celebrations in Brazil. Black musicians formed groups called samba schools in the 1930s. The samba schools have floats and parades at Carnaval. Everyone dances to the African rhythm of the samba. Another popular dance in Brazil is the bossa nova.

▲ *A samba performer*

The Future of Brazil

▲ *Native American children*

People in Brazil live in two very different ways. Some Brazilians who live in or near cities have good jobs and can buy what they need. Most people in remote villages have little or no money. They can barely feed their families. They even burn rain forest land and try to farm. But people all over the world want to protect the rain forests of Brazil.

If you visit Brazil, you will learn more about this special Latin American country. Then as you leave, you will probably say "*Obrigado*! Thank you! I liked my visit to Brazil."

▲ *Children at a rural school*

Glossary

continent—one of Earth's seven great landmasses

equator—an imaginary line around the middle of the Earth

gaucho—a Brazilian cowboy

highlands—hilly land

lowlands—forested land that is lower than the land around it

pampa—grass-covered flat land

plains—flat land

plateau—high, flat land with steep sides

Did You Know?

- In parts of Brazil, some children must work in the fields or in factories to help feed their families.

- The modern city of Brasília is shaped like an airplane.

- Brazil produces about one-fifth of the world's coffee beans.

At a Glance

Official name: *República Federativo do Brasil* (Federative Republic of Brazil)

Capital: Brasília

Official language: Portuguese

National song: *"Hino Nacional do Brasil"* ("Brazilian National Anthem")

Area: 3,286,488 square miles (8,511,965 square kilometers)

Highest point: Pico da Neblina 9,888 feet (3,016 meters) above sea level

Lowest point: Sea level along the coast

Population: 169,430,000 (1998 estimate)

Head of government: President

Money: Real

Important Dates

1400s Europeans explore and settle in Brazil.

1500 Pedro Álvares Cabral claims Brazil for Portugal.

1822 Brazil declares independence from Portugal.

1888 Slaves in Brazil are freed.

1960 Brazil's capital is moved from Rio de Janeiro to Brasília.

1988 Brazil adopts a new constitution.

Want to Know More?

At the Library

Dawson, Zoe. *Brazil*. Austin, Tex.: Raintree Steck-Vaughn, 1996.

Haverstock, Nathan A. *Brazil*. Minneapolis: Lerner Publications Co., 1997.

Morrison, Marion. *Brazil*. Austin, Tex.: Raintree Steck-Vaughn, 1997.

On the Web

The Kayapo: A Disappearing Culture

http://gbms01.uwgb.edu/~galta/mrr/kayapo/

For information about the ceremonies, myths, and beliefs of this tribal culture in Brazil

Oxfam's World: Brazil

http://www.oxfam.org.uk/coolplanet/kidsweb/world/Brazil/brazhome. htm

For details about life in Brazil today, including the people, history, and geography

Through the Mail

Brazilian Embassy

3006 Massachusetts Avenue, N.W.

Washington, DC 20008

For information about the country

On the Road

Brazilian-American Chamber of Commerce

22 West 48th Street, Suite 404

New York, NY 10036

212/575-9030

To find out about visiting Brazil

Index

About the Author

Shirley W. Gray received her bachelor's degree in education from the University of Mississippi and her master's degree in technical writing from the University of Arkansas. She teaches writing and works as a scientific writer and editor. Shirley W. Gray lives with her husband and two sons in Little Rock, Arkansas.